Authentically Successful

Lessons from Your Higher Self

Unlock Lasting Abundance, Joy and Courage

Metaphysical Self-Help, Book 3

By Elena G. Rivers

All rights reserved. No part of this publication may be reproduced, stored in a retrieval system, or transmitted, in any form or by any means, electronic, mechanical, photocopying, recording, or otherwise, without the author and the publishers' prior written permission.

The scanning, uploading, and distributing this book via the Internet or any other means without the author's permission are illegal and punishable by law. Please purchase only authorized electronic editions and do not participate in or encourage electronic piracy of copyrighted materials.

Elena G. Rivers © Copyright 2023 - All rights reserved.

ISBN: 9781800950825

Legal Notice:

This book is copyright protected—it is for personal use only.

Disclaimer Notice:

Please note that the information contained in this book is for inspirational and entertainment purposes only. Every attempt has been made to provide accurate, up-to-date, and completely reliable information. However, no warranties of any kind are expressed or implied. Readers acknowledge that the author is not engaging in the rendering of legal, financial, health, medical, or professional advice. By reading this book, the reader agrees that under no circumstances are we responsible for any losses, direct or indirect, which are incurred due to the use of the information contained within this book, including, but not limited to, errors, omissions, or inaccuracies. The information provided in this book is for entertainment and inspirational purposes only. If you are struggling with serious problems, including chronic illness, mental or financial instability, or legal issues, please consult with your local registered health care, financial or legal professional. This book is not a substitute for professional or legal advice; it is designed as a collection of spiritual and philosophical concepts to motivate and uplift you on your quest for success and self-actualization.

Contents

From the Author – It's Time to Clear Out What Has Been Holding You Back and Manifest the Life You Love, Desire, and Deserve 6

Introduction and a Warm, Heartful Welcome from Your Higher Self 14

Chapter 1 – Lesson 1 19

Manifestation is a Lifestyle You Choose to Embody 24/7, and I'll Show You How (It Feels Good and Effortless!) 19

Chapter 2 - Lesson 2 33

Becoming Successful by Writing Your Own Sacred Playbook 33

Chapter 3 - Lesson 3 55

Making Friends with Fear (Instead of Fighting It!). The Perfect Integration Process for Unlimited Courage. 55

Join Our Manifestation Newsletter and Get a Free eBook 63

More by Elena 65

From the Author – It's Time to Clear Out What Has Been Holding You Back and Manifest the Life You Love, Desire, and Deserve

Hello Beautiful Soul! Thank You so much for stopping by and choosing this book.

I genuinely believe you were guided to do so! Why? Because your Higher Self wrote this book for you, and it chose me to be the Messenger and Connector. I'm deeply grateful to be sharing these high-frequency, life-changing messages with you because it aligns with my life mission- to empower as many people as possible to manifest the true, authentically abundant life they deserve and desire, one soul at a time!

Our planet is undergoing an exciting, energetic shift at the moment. We are transitioning from fear-based, limiting mindsets to love-based empowerment of unlimited possibilities created for the highest good of all! That shift alone can transform all areas of our lives and how we show up for ourselves and others. You can infuse whatever you do with love and empowerment, inspiring others to transform as well. Love is the highest vibration we can experience in this physical existence, and we came here to unleash its power as much as we can.

We are stepping into the best versions of ourselves every day while connecting to our Higher Selves. This is precisely what this book is all about. All you need to do is to relax and read it with your heart while allowing yourself to uncover your own unique version of success.

We are finally ready to move beyond old, outdated concepts of the same success formula for everyone.

Instead, we are ready to honor our uniqueness, choose what works for us and what is authentic, and embody our truth for our highest good. At the same time, we inspire others to do the same. Because seeing others succeed in their own unique way, makes us happy. There's no more separation and no more competition. We replace the word: "competition" with: "collaboration" , "completion" and "creation".

We all feel whole, complete, and unique. So how can we "compete" with someone else? Everyone is on their own journey for the highest good of all.

Yes, the old, outdated success concepts may have worked for some. But many were left empty-handed and deeply discouraged because they wasted all their time and energy chasing something that wasn't aligned with their truth. Instead, they were pursuing someone else's goals and definition of success. I, too, used to be one of those individuals, and as a result, my soul suffered tremendously. However, the realization that my time was better spent on tuning into my inner wisdom and helping others do the same gave my old "suffering" the meaning I needed to transition to a new way of thinking, feeling, and being.

My old self lost herself chasing someone else's standards and working so hard that her health was at serious risk...only to end up unhappy and not as abundant as she'd initially intended. Quite the opposite...

But this is how she realized the hidden truth of manifesting success...

It all starts with knowing who you are, which is one of the intentions this little, magic-infused book holds inside.

Your Higher Self knows what's good for you. And it knew how to convey its most powerful and love-filled messages so that whoever reads this book can feel empowered. It doesn't matter who you are and where you're from. This book aims to connect you with your true, authentic essence to help you create success that feels good.

It also simplifies the success manifestation process. It sees it as a lifestyle you embody to get the desired results. And it doesn't want to overwhelm you with an endless ocean of information you feel like you to have to keep putting into small buckets full of holes...ending up frustrated and seeing no progress...

(The first lesson from your Higher Self in chapter 1 illustrates this beautifully!).

Another thing this book will help you transform (thanks to Your Higher Self!) is your self-talk. Your self-talk forms an integral part of your life. Whether you're conscious of it or not, you're always talking to yourself.

The big question that makes all the difference is: is your self-talk in alignment with your true desires?

Does it make you feel good, full of hope, energy, love, and inspiration?

Is your self-talk like an inspiring personal coach that offers guidance and motivation filled with love?

Or perhaps it's full of voices that are not even yours....

They come from old paradigms that are no longer relevant to your current mission (such as creating authentic success from a place of love!)

You want to create something truly yours, manifest your goals, and positively impact this planet.

This is why these empowering messages from your Higher Self are so important. Your Higher Self vibrates so high that it can't even relate to your self-imposed limitations or negative self-talk.

Reading this book alone and consciously choosing to soak in all the beautiful conversations with Your Higher Self will help you shift your self-talk pretty much on autopilot. So, the voices in your head will be different. You will reach a totally new vibration and frequency, new ideas and powerful solutions...

This is a good thing because connecting to Your Higher Self gives you access to a new level of consciousness.

As Albert Einstein once said:

"No problem can be solved from the same level of consciousness that created it."

So, by saturating your self-talk with messages from your Higher Self, you automatically access a new level of awareness.

By staying connected to your Higher Self, your Best Self, you access the best solutions created specifically for you. You feel more grounded, relaxed and at ease, so taking mindful action from a new, aligned paradigm is easy and fun.

Read with an open heart and set an intention to keep peeling off the old, negative layers, one step at a time. My personal recommendation is that you read this book more than once. Before reading it, you may focus on one intention, to move closer to a desired outcome.

For example: "Find an investment opportunity that is right for me," or: "Attract meaningful and beautiful friendships," or: "Create a healthy lifestyle I love."

Then relax, read, clear out any old negative energies and mindsets holding you back and make these empowering and joyful conversations with Your Higher Self your new normal!

Because manifesting is your birthright. You are worthy of creating a beautiful life just because you are, just because you exist. I know you've come a long way to find this message, but now it makes more and more sense.

You're reaching a new chapter where past obstacles are transformed into life lessons and opportunities. You are becoming a wise student and teacher, ready to help and empower yourself while tuning into your full potential to pay it forward and help others.

Even if you don't know your purpose work yet, don't worry. Instead, enjoy the journey of self-exploration and be grateful for every step you choose to go through.

Remember that staying committed to self-growth and self-discovery can be your purpose too. By knowing more about yourself and choosing to be guided by your Higher Self, your work will automatically have more meaning. And because of your new attitude, don't be surprised if new opportunities come your way.

So, it's time to get started...

It's time to reach a state of joy and inspiration. And it's time to take meaningful and inspired action that feels good and gets us closer to our desired destination (while still loving the journey!).

What is inspiration or inspired action anyway? When we look closer at this beautiful word, we can see the similarities between the words: s*pirit* and *inspiration.*

Because inspired action is taken IN SPIRIT. It all starts with going inwards and accessing that part of you with all the answers you need to find permanent success and happiness.

Oh, and one more thing. If you've read any of my books before, especially the *Heart-Based Manifesting* series, you know that I always encourage readers to read my writings with their hearts as much as possible. Set an intention to be more in your heart as you read this book. Notice how good it feels when you're more in your heart (and how it helps your mind to open and quickly embrace new ideas).

Thank you once again for choosing my book, and happy reading.

With love and gratitude,

Elena

Your friend and guide in conscious manifesting

PS. As an additional resource, I'd like to invite you to join my LOA newsletter and download a free copy of my Law of Attraction Workbook – *How to Raise Your Vibration in 5 Days or Less*.

This bonus offering includes a free eBook + audiobook (in case you're to busy to read; I know what it's like to sign up for free eBooks that never get read and live a limited and disempowered life somewhere in your inbox, lol!).

Visit: www.LOAforSuccess.com/newsletter

Any tech problems, please email: info@LOAforSuccess.com

Introduction and a Warm, Heartful Welcome from Your Higher Self

Hello Beautiful Soul! Before we dive into this program, I wanted to properly introduce myself and briefly tell you what you can expect and how I can help you.

Yes, I know you know I am your Higher Self.

But do you know what I think about you?

If something like: "Oh no, if she/he is my Higher Self, then I must be their Lower Self" crossed your beautiful mind for even a second, please let it go now. Erase, delete, release!

Because you are NOT my lower self. You are the Highest of my Highest Self, and we work together as a team. Because as a team, we are even more powerful.

OK, so let me guess. You are probably wondering why I am calling you the Highest of my Highest Self?

You probably can't comprehend why because your logical mind is confused thinking:

"Is this some kind of a joke? How can my Higher Self suddenly lower themselves and be below me? After all, I am connecting to it to get the answers I need to be more successful."

As Your Higher Self, let me explain that I operate from different paradigms. And there are no "levels" here.

It's also a good lesson for you to understand how some old paradigms can hold you back...

So, back to your original state of confusion. I call you the Highest of my Highest Self because I'm coming to you from the future. And it's thanks to You that I got to where I am today. Everything you've done to this point in your life helped us shine our full potential. You DID EVERYTHING RIGHT. Whether you realize it or not. So please release all that shame, guilt, or resentment. Let us feel a bit lighter, OK? Good, so...

Everything led us to this point; from here, we can only keep transforming more and more.

Perhaps you sometimes feel like you did something wrong. Once again, release all that guilt now. I learned so much from you and what you still perceive as "mistakes" (but I call them *sacred lessons*).

You see, the lessons I acquired and the reason you call me Your Higher Self is that I've been learning from you this whole time.

But for now, we are primarily concerned about working together - You, the Highest of my Highest Self) and I – the entity you refer to as Your Higher Self.

We go through life together, and together we shine.

You need to know that I am coming to you from the future. And the way I perceive time is totally different than you do because you live by the linear concepts of time (which is great, thanks to that you can attend an important meeting on time, so please keep that ability, haha).

But I live a non-linear manifestation lifestyle.

Like I said, I'm coming to you from what you perceive as "future". So please stick to that concept because I know it's fun. It will also be more effective if you see it as such.

I, however, can see and live everything as happening now in this very moment. What you see as past, present, and future. Everything is *now* to me. And everything is good, everything is perfect. I see perfection in everything; my natural state is bliss and gratitude.

OK, so what does my way of thinking bring to the table, or better said, the table of success for you here on Earth?

Well, the most important one is that it soothes your inner state. Because as Your Higher Self, I've already experienced a zillion beautiful manifestations that perhaps are still on your desires list. And I can help you manifest faster. I can help you change your mindset and energy.

Oh, and don't worry because I can't mess with your future. I can only shift things in your life in a way you wholeheartedly desire; in other words, the changes I can help you make can only be positive.

And these changes will start taking place immediately and automatically if you choose to. But please remember that they will first start taking place within you.

The primary purpose of this book is to help you change your mindset and energy in alignment with your Higher Self (that is me, and I am an expert here, and I feel like you know you can trust me!).

Now, I already mentioned that what you call your past "failures," "mistakes," or "bad decisions," or even unfulfilled manifestations never got me off track. In fact, they made me into your Higher Self (and they also made me realize I should call you the Highest of my Higher Self). You didn't do anything wrong, and everything is happening exactly as it should.

I'm not saying this just to make you feel better (although I am here to make you feel good) but to help you align your current perspective (of what you may see as setbacks and limitations) with a greater universal truth.

And the way I see those "limitations" is as our most incredible power. Something that qualifies us to be our own Team Successful. Authentically successful. So, no more labels such as: "bad." Where I come from, everything is perfect and divine.

If, for whatever reason, you still encounter those negative thoughts, promise yourself to love yourself through them and then release them. Take a few deep breaths in. As you inhale, visualize beautiful healing light of love, wisdom, and success entering your body. As you breathe out, say: "release, because I choose to be free!"

Your focus needs to be crystal clear on what you desire. But, never feel bad for experiencing negative thoughts. They are merely an indicator that something needs to be released and you're about to reach a new level of inner freedom. It's a never-ending process you need to be committed to as you go through your journey of self-growth and creating authentic success.

So, now that we're both on the same page let's start our little divinely-inspired program on how to be authentically successful....

Chapter 1 – Lesson 1

Manifestation is a Lifestyle You Choose to Embody 24/7, and I'll Show You How (It Feels Good and Effortless!)

Here's the biggest lesson you need to embody if you want to be successful. Once you've embodied it, nobody will ever take it away from you, and you will always be able to shift to more desirable realities.

Imagine that beautiful sense of freedom that your success will never depend on any third party, the economy, or the government. Yes, of course, some outside changes may temporarily influence your life to some degree, it's never a bad idea to stay up-to-date. We're not talking about living in oblivion or hiding in a cave.

However, the only person fully responsible for your success is you and only you. Sometimes, certain outside changes may be a bit tough and disheartening. And every now and then, they will happen. But with what you're about to learn in this chapter, you will always be able to shift to more empowering states and timelines while maintaining inner peace and balance. You will feel peaceful and in charge.

It all starts with the relationship you have with your subconscious mind. Imagine it as a printer. You give it a command, and it prints. It's all it does; it's really that simple.

So, what are you going to print? Your desired outcomes and realities or endless complaints about what's wrong with your current job, neighborhood, and taxes?

You can always focus on growth and success. And you can succeed despite negative realities that may be surrounding you.

Let's take it one step further. In our imagination, we are always safe and can do whatever we want. And it's thanks to our imagination that we can maintain a calm inner state and be unshakable and resilient...

So, imagine that your beautiful subconscious mind is like a newspaper or a magazine...

And it simply prints what you tell it to print. You are a chief editor. So, how can you tell it to print your desired reality?

Be very mindful of how you talk to yourself and how you treat yourself. This is the manifestation lifestyle mindset I want you to master. And, in fact, I learned it from you when you were doing it unconsciously and perhaps not in a very empowering way, to say the least...

You know all those little instances when things were not going your way, and you just kept complaining to yourself and others. And your private newspapers and magazines were full of headlines such as:

"You are a loser, nobody likes you, you will never succeed, you have no skills...!".

You unconsciously kept printing the same old reality. Then, you learned about the Law of Attraction, and your first instinct was to learn about its techniques. And these are great.

But here's the problem, you were doing the techniques on the outside. Kind of like launching a short-lived positivity attack on the outside world. But then, you were secretly printing out the same negative headlines and entire articles dedicated to what you perceived as failure and what you thought was wrong with you.

You discovered scripting and money affirmations. And these are great tools for sure, but they must align with your manifesting lifestyle. Back then, you had no clue, so every day, you got pumped out for 30 minutes imagining and writing about your perfect lifestyle...

You got excited, and you manifested some good things here and there.

But then you stubbornly kept printing those ugly, negative headlines, creating something I call *counter-manifesting*.

And to watch it happen from my dimension, sometimes I can't clearly say if it's funny or sad or both. I guess it's a bit crazy because why not just focus on your desired outcomes? Why not print your desired reality? Even if it still does not fully match your current one, it's an illusion anyway, remember I live a non-linear time lifestyle...

OK, now I am probably confusing you or making you feel bad...

And my job contract clearly says I am here to empower you, and it feels good to do so, so please don't take any of my words as an offense. If anything, take it as a joke and laugh. Because adding humor to your manifestation process and lifestyle is good.

Why take everything so seriously? Yes, you definitely want to stay committed to your positive vision. But that doesn't mean you always have to be so serious.

So, back to those negative headlines and entire negative articles you stubbornly kept printing while doing your cute little LOA techniques and half-hearted affirmations...

The headlines you were secretly printing were the main reason you felt stuck. There was no alignment. You wanted one thing on the outside but then, your inner state kept printing self-imposed limitations such as: "It will take too long", "I will never make it", "It's soo much to learn"...

How about changing your inner printer, or how about creating your own internal publishing company that you fully own? Decide what to print. Stick to it.

Here's where to take your inspiration from...First of all, don't get inspired by your current circumstances unless you fully love them (if you do, then yes, create gratitude headlines and let the Universe know you desire more of that good stuff).

In most cases, you will need to be more creative and write headlines that reflect what you want, or at least get you closer to what you want with confidence and ease. These headlines are designed to make you feel good and focused on your goal.

And you can also write entire articles about your success and add beautiful pictures. Because whether you realize it or not, you're always writing, visualizing, or affirming something in your mind. But now it's time to be in charge. Yes, I won't deny that some mental discipline will be required, and in the beginning, it may feel a bit hard, but it's only because nobody taught you this before.

Examples of good headlines you can create in your mind:

-"How I turned obstacles into opportunities and manifested the business of my dreams!".

-"How, even though everyone told me it would never be possible in the current economy, I bought my dream apartment, and I love it!".

Some headlines may also focus on getting closer to your goal or manifesting a specific solution or someone who can help you.

Example:

-"How I always manifest great professionals. For example, the real estate agent I attracted into my life helped me so much. Now I know I can manifest my house with ease!".

I call these: *little transition headlines.*

For example, if creating bold headlines doesn't feel good to you now, and for some reason, your mind says: "Yeah, right, I wish it was true" you can start with transition headlines.

So, instead of creating a headline such as: "I have a six-figure business and easily manifest new, soul-aligned clients."

You can create a headline such as:

"I have now successfully manifested my first client. I am so happy and grateful that I have a great part-time business I love. I manifest extra money and help people; it's great!"

There's no right or wrong. Simply go inwards and start practicing. Start re-editing and re-printing these old negative headlines. It's a great thing to do in your spare time. You can do it during meditation, as you work out, or create a relaxation routine around it.

Please don't tell me you don't have time. Because you're continuously printing something anyways...now it's time to do it consciously. So, instead of verbally reacting to your current reality, you create a new one, all from a state of peace, balance, and calm confidence.

Because the fastest way to manifest success is to print positive headlines and when you get used to it, saturate your subconscious mind with positive articles about you and your accomplishments.

In your mind, you're safe and can print whatever you want.

One thing I'll add, just in case. When I talk about writing and printing positive headlines, I refer to a mental and emotional activity you do in your mind. It can also be a spiritual activity if you talk to yourself or a Higher Power. But the main thing is: you don't talk about it to others (unless they practice a manifestation lifestyle are your trusted mentors and you're on the same page and share the lessons learned). But, in most cases, the golden rule is – keep your inner work to yourself.

So here are a few ways you can choose to embody the manifestation lifestyle starting now...

Let's say you desire to manifest more money and abundance into your life. And you come across someone wealthy. As always, you have different choices (different ways to write and print your headlines).

You can choose to get triggered by someone's wealth and decide to say negative things about them. But when doing so, you're also printing negative headlines about your own money desires...And these are not positive...

(Side note - if that wealthy person really did something dishonest, just release them from your awareness. They are not your concern or example to follow. Say: "release, release". And move on. Sooner or later, their karma will take care of them. But it's not up to us to be their judge.)

Instead, you can choose to print positive headlines such as: "I am discovering meaningful and honest ways to manifest more money and abundance, the Universe is sending me success stories and inspiration. I know I can do it!".

You can use an example of someone dishonest to help you focus on the opposite. And you can even say: "Thank you because your example shows me what I do not want to become. "

Another example: someone cuts you off on the road.

You can use it as a source of positive motivation and focus. You can say: "I am so happy and grateful that there are still some good and careful drivers out there. That rude driver reminded me how good it feels to do things the right way without putting anyone in danger".

BOOM, done. So much better than complaining.

Everything can happen for you and become your positive fuel or motivation. Choose the lenses through which you see the world wisely. Because you can!

Now, your subconscious mind will start absorbing that positive message, and you will soon manifest positive proof, such as people who do meaningful things and treat others with respect.

So, now let's take a look at another scenario. You want to manifest wealth by doing what you love. And you've just seen a person doing something similar and they're wildly successful.

What headlines are you going to print? That of jealousy or disbelief? Or perhaps outdated headlines like: "They must have done something dishonest."

Or: "Why can other people succeed and I can't?"

Let me be blunt here. Yes, I know I am your Higher Self, and maybe you expected me to speak some ultra-spiritual language; who knows. But I am here to do my job!

So here's the truth. Your subconscious mind is like... an intelligent idiot (please note, I am not calling you an idiot, just using this comparison to illustrate how the subconscious mind works and how to use it to your advantage). If you keep saturating it with headlines like: "Money is bad. Others are successful, but I am not", it will keep printing out more and more of the same.

Yes, some affirmations, vision boards, and scripting on the side may temporarily improve your situation. Or improve it only a tiny bit but never really help you make significant changes.

Remember, I know the fastest way. And the fastest way is to write and print positive headlines of how you desire things to be. *All the time!* It's so much fun, and you can never lose, trust me on that one. Just keep practicing and experimenting.

Then infuse your new headlines with positive feelings. Don't attach negative emotions such as impatience, jealousy, or anger to your headlines. If you have problems with feeling positive, then just enter a neutral state.

So, you have two choices here- our positive (authentic) state. Such a state is easy to access when you meditate, think about the things you love, listen to theta state-inducing music, are out in nature, dance, sing, read feel-good stuff, or whatever makes you feel good...

Just don't pretend you feel positive when you don't. Be honest with yourself.

Luckily you have another option you can choose, and it's to be in a neutral state. You can visualize deleting those negative headlines and seeing a blank page.

So now, here's the best part. The Universe gives you a fantastic opportunity to print positive headlines 24/7.

And these headlines don't have to be perfectly formulated or grammatically correct.

Sometimes you can use simple words or quick visualizations. Oh, and if you're wondering when you should write your headlines or for how long...there's no specific answer or formula. Just be very aware throughout the day and remember that everything happens for you if you choose to. In your mind, you're always safe.

Also, don't overdo anything. It's not that now you have to sit in your imaginary printing company 24/7 and keep printing positive headlines. Don't see it as a technique you have to use, but more as a state of mind you embody or a lifestyle you choose to live.

The next time you catch your negative self-talk...go to your imaginary printing company and change the headlines about yourself as fast as you can.

The next time someone says something negative, don't be too quick to react and perpetuate the same old reality. Instead, quickly sneak out to your imaginary publishing company and create a new headline.

"I am so happy and grateful that people always listen to me with respect and value my advice."

Well, this is my new headline to give you a simple example.

And sometimes, I like to write about myself in the third person...

"This beautiful and highly skilled Higher Self has yet another amazing talent, she knows how to connect with people, and they always value her advice".

Sometimes, the first-person plural does it for me (it's so nice to team up with you!).

So, let's write a nice headline about us:

"We are a great team, and we always attract great people who listen to us, and they love what we have to say!".

These examples of everyday situations should inspire you, and changes can come quite quickly. The first one will be more peace of mind and a feeling of joy and playfulness. You will really see your reality as your playground!

To sum up, instead of reacting to what you don't want and don't like, choose to mentally respond to what you desire through creating positive headlines. Easy peasy, right? Just remember to remember my dear!

Now your homework is to become more aware of what inner headlines you're currently printing. Swiftly adjust them to more meaningful and positive ones. Stay focused on what you desire, the best way to get there, or any positive step in the right direction. As you keep printing positive headlines, your reality will begin to shift. It's so much fun, so let's start printing what we want, shall we?

Chapter 2 - Lesson 2

Becoming Successful by Writing Your Own Sacred Playbook

If you want to manifest authentic success, more often than not, you may want to consider doing the opposite of what you're told to do. So, whatever definitions of success you are surrounded by, get into the habit of questioning them and creating your own. Because you have the final say! It's as simple as saying: "yes" or "no" in your mind. If you see something you don't want to follow, simply walk away. Visualize a big "stop" sign in your mind, or say "cancel, cancel." That will free your mind and your precious energy to stay focused on what you love, your true path.

At the same time, if you see something you like, for example, someone doing something very inspiring, embrace that feeling fully. Instruct your subconscious mind with positive statements such as: "Yes, this is what I like; please send me more success stories like this one."

Oh, and of course, now you know how to print positive headlines and be creative, so never forget what you've learned in the previous chapter and embody it fully.

Creating your own definition of success may be stressful at times, especially if you go against the grain and against what's perceived as the standard opinion of everyone or almost everyone around you.

But remember the golden rule, your primary focus needs to be on what you desire and where you're going (while being grateful for where you're at). So, don't waste your energy trying to over-explain yourself others. Your main job is to stay focused on your own transformation, not to keep building walls of explanations around your choices.

So, here's the most critical part of this chapter because none of the techniques shared above will be effective if you don't know your definition of success and don't have your own sacred success playbook.

This is why I wanted to talk to you. I knew I could help you create your definition of success, or at least get you in the habit of making it, by feeling empowered to think for yourself and live according to your own life philosophy.

Oh, and one more thing, just to be sure we're on the same page. Creating your own definition of success and rules is not an event but a continuous process reflecting your self-growth and self-awareness journey. You are the only writer and editor of your success playbook, so you can continuously adapt your rules if needed. The most rewarding part will occur when you realize how your reality reflects your inner success playbook. When you reach this beautiful moment, you will wonder how you could ever live without it! But never beat yourself up over the things you didn't do (because you weren't awake.)

Remind yourself that it's all about learning, and you can always catch up.

So, instead of launching a poorly organized and haphazard attack on the outside circumstances, start by going inwards and getting clear on what success really is to you. And whenever you get an idea, question it several times by asking yourself: "Is this idea coming from my heart, or is it something I picked up from others, but it doesn't serve me?"

Of course, I'm not saying that other people can't inspire you. Your only job here is to scan your inner feelings. Does a given definition of success feel good and inspiring to you? Or perhaps you fear peer and societal pressure and want to pursue something just because you don't believe in yourself?

Remember that you now have Your Higher Self (that is me!) at your disposal, and I've already taught you how to secretly print those beautiful headlines to keep you empowered and focused on the positive, even if everyone around you doesn't seem to get you. Remember that you're always safe, and there's no obligation to share your vision with anyone, especially if they are not supportive.

So, let's go inwards and allow our dreams to expand...

Where I come from (your future), I can tell you that you did amazingly well, my beautiful Highest of My Highest Self, just because you decided to reclaim your power.

And from now on, you think, feel and act intentionally to live the life you desire and deserve. You started by re-writing your inner script (your own authentic success playbook.)

Most definitions of success you get from other people have probably told you that it's all about money and career. Because when you make more money, you will be happy and finally feel good.

Now yes, these are important in the physical plane of existence. And you can undoubtedly manifest a great career where you feel fulfilled and greatly compensated for your work.

But there is so much more to success...

There is also love, well-being, friendships, spirituality, freedom, and contribution...

And having work that doesn't feel like work to you because you love what you do...so why not have it all?

It all starts with a simple decision and inner shift so that you can create success in all areas of your life.

I am sure you resonate with my definition because now that we have connected, it's also yours!

Please don't get overwhelmed and don't escape into any states of unworthiness or "other people can have it all, but I can't." mindsets. Remember that you create your own script, so please don't delegate this critical task to other people.

Here's a simple mental and energetic exercise you can start doing right here and now...You can do it in your mind or as a written manifestation exercise in your journal.

The most important thing you need to embrace to be authentically successful in all areas of your life while speeding up your manifestations is the unique feeling you experience as you think about your success.

Start with just one area of your life you desire to supercharge. Let's take money as an example. As you think about the money you'd like to manifest, experience the feeling behind your money-focused thought.

What would you do with your money? Where would you live? Would your life change a lot, or just a little?

Both are fine, just remember to stay true to yourself and follow what feels good and authentic to you, there's no right or wrong.

Now, start adding more areas of your life to your desired feeling. As you do this exercise, you can visualize, talk to yourself, and print positive headlines, whatever feels good to you and your beautiful imagination.

To recap what we've just covered and to add new steps:

1. Start with one area of your life, something you desire to supercharge right now, for example: money, raising your income, or any financial situation. Always stay focused on the desired outcome and the feeling behind it.
2. Embrace that beautiful feeling as much as possible and allow your imagination to guide you.

Now, start adding other areas of your life, for example, health & wellness. Ask yourself: How does that area of my life feel now that I make more money?

For example, you can see yourself indulging in your favorite self-care activities, such as juicing organic vegetables, yoga, or self-care rituals. Intend to stay focused on your positive feelings. Is it feeling well-taken care of and healthy? Is it the feeling of freedom because now you can buy delicious and nutritious foods or attend yoga classes that you've always wanted to try?

3. Repeat with other areas of your life, for example, personal growth.

   Ask your imagination:

   "Now that I manifest more money, how does it positively impact my self-growth?" Perhaps you can visualize yourself attending your dream seminars, talking to your favorite mentors or meeting like-minded souls during beautiful retreats you have always wanted to attend.

4. Once again, repeat with as many areas of your life as you want to. For example, personal relationships. Now that you keep manifesting more and more money, how does it affect your personal relationships? Perhaps you can see yourself helping those you love. Maybe you would love to help a loved one get a college degree? Once again, embrace the feeling behind it...

Well done! Because now you know how to impress your subconscious mind with your desire on different levels. Your subconscious mind may find it challenging to process numbers (such as how much money you desire to manifest). Yes, these are all great goals to have and can serve as a compass. It's also great to have milestones that motivate you to keep going.

But your subconscious mind loves the language of the feeling of what you desire, and that feeling needs to be positive. Now, I'm not saying we need to always feel super excited and pumped to a level that almost feels superficial. I already told you that sometimes a simple, neutral state can be much more beneficial. We don't want to get high only to end up low because we feel like we are deceiving ourselves.

So, back to a simple exercise we did; its primary purpose was to show you how to talk to your beautiful subconscious mind. Think about all the benefits to it, such as:

-you associate money with positive images and situations, and your subconscious hears:

"Money- good, money- health, money- love, OK, let's print- a new reality- money-good- more of that please- search- for money- opportunities."

Your subconscious mind is like a search engine. When you program it with clear instructions (images of what you want across different areas of your life so that you can experience the same feeling in different ways), it will start searching for proof in its "search engine". And so, your reality will begin to reflect that search. As a result, you may get an idea to manifest more money, or more ideas will find you.

Your main job is to stay focused on what you want by translating your desire (such as desired income in dollars or your local currency) to a multi-sensory language of your subconscious mind, saturated with images, sounds, smells, and feelings...

But what if you're not focused on money right now? Yes, I know, I know. I've mentioned that the traditional definition of success, which is only about money and career, is not enough...

So, let's repeat the same exercise with something different...

Start with one specific area of your life, such as:

-health and fitness;

-spiritual experiences;

-relationship with your parents;

-relationship with your spouse;

-manifesting new friendships;

For our little "presentation," let's do...spiritual experiences. Let's say you desire to manifest a strong connection with your angels, ancestors, spirit guides, or whatever Higher Power you believe in. You want to stay connected to that power to experience many beautiful and magical moments in your life and access guidance and healing whenever you need direction.

So, embrace that feeling. You are always guided. You are always protected. And as your spiritual experiences keep amplifying, your life gets better and better every day.

Let's tie this beautiful spiritual manifestation into other areas of your life. You will be surprised how creative we can get and how fast your life can change when you embrace the "I can have it all" mindset while making friends with your subconscious mind...

Now you are always guided and protected and feel empowered to follow your purpose (or be guided to get closer to it). And you're not afraid to make that first important step to shift your career and manifest more money because you know you are safe. You have an entire team of angels, spirit guides, and your ancestors wanting to help you. So, you can release all that stress, worry, fear and doubt...How does it feel? Can you see yourself doing things differently and making more significant moves simply because you feel safe, guided, and protected?

What about your health and wellness?

Now that you worry less because you know you have manifested an excellent spiritual connection and have a beautiful team of divine beings ready to support you, you have more energy and zest for life. You love yourself more and more, so self-care feels natural. You intuitively know the healthy foods and habits that are good for you and create a healthy lifestyle you enjoy.

Your spiritual connection helps you be more calm, peaceful, and present...so think and feel how it can positively impact your relationships. You become a person of peace and develop a magnetic aura that people feel attracted to!

Your spiritual connection helps you stay away from toxic people without even trying, simply because you're on a new vibration. You also feel inspired to forgive because you know you deserve to create new space for the magical experiences that are yet to come.

Congratulations, you have just impressed your subconscious mind in a very powerful way. Because you've spoken its language. And another benefit for you is that it helped you reach a place of deep peace and relaxation.

It's pretty easy and fun, right? Imagine what can happen when you start doing it every day...

The more you practice it, the better you get. Eventually, you will develop your own process. After all, you are the Highest of my Highest Self, and you know exactly what to do.

As you keep practicing your subconscious mind's communication and speak its language, you may also want to develop your own life map.

You are already familiar with the term: "different areas of your life", and you may have noticed that different writers or coaches have different terminology.

Because everyone is different and everyone expresses their truth in their unique way. Now, here's the next mission for you...Since you are the writer of your life and your own coach, feel free to develop whatever terminology feels good to you.

Start by listing different areas of life that are important to you. Do it in your own way. Yes, you can use lessons from other people as inspiration. But don't just copy what they created, and don't just blindly follow through. Always test and question everything according to your life philosophy and preferences.

So, take a piece of paper and divide your life into different categories important to you. Notice how they nicely complement one another. But don't overwhelm yourself with too many. Manifesting authentic success and inner work should be more about feelings, not so much about more mental activities and things you have to do... Remember the language of your subconscious mind. <u>Feel to grow rich in all areas of your life!</u>

I will give you an example to get you started.

Different areas of life that are important to me:

-Meaningful work that is fulfilling and pays well;

-Healthy and fit body that gives me unstoppable energy;

-Kind, loving, and supportive friends who love me for who I am;

-Highly developed spirituality and intuition.

Your positive memories of your future will help you make your own life map, and you will quickly realize how all areas of your life are interconnected and that you can indeed have it all. Even if your main focus now is money or career, as you go deep within and talk to your subconscious mind, you also tie in other areas of your life. So, your life keeps getting better and better. You feel more energized and connected. And going after your goals feels joyful and fun, just like manifesting should feel. One area of your life fuels another. Your daily actions are mindful and intentional and lead to a result you desire to manifest. You feel empowered knowing that you are moving in the right direction, and you're also enjoying your journey and feel grateful for every step you discover.

Now, let's dedicate the rest of this chapter to redefining your version of success.

Here's the most critical divine and authentic success formula:

Go inwards and question everything...there is nothing wrong with questioning, even your own questions or popular opinions.

Settling for a popular opinion without questioning it is being reactive not proactive. It's like lowering your vibration just to fit in. But now that you are aware of this common pitfall, you can choose more empowering options and create your own rules.

The sad truth is that many people are not very happy with their lives (which, for many, is a starting point to change something, but some just remain where they are and choose to complain).

Why would you want to do what most people do? Why not choose infinite empowerment instead?

Why not create your own definition of success and stick to it?

Remember that now you know how to stay empowered and focused on what you want by printing positive headlines.

You must formulate your own beliefs around different areas of your life, don't just repeat what you were taught by your family, teachers, or mentors. Even if you feel like you've learned a lot from them and are grateful for their teachings, always dive deep and keep developing your own version of your own opinions and beliefs.

One of the best questions you can ask yourself is: "Is this belief/goal/opinion really mine? Is it coming from my heart? Or is it something I just mindlessly repeat from others?"

Be confident in your abilities and act on your own authority. Don't do what everyone else does out of fear that you can't follow your way.

Authentically successful people take calculated risks, so it's not about being irrational or illogical and risking your health or life savings. It's simply about allowing yourself to expand your comfort zone. Just like going to the gym, there is a bit of discomfort and discipline related to growth. But eventually, it becomes your lifestyle, and if you were guided to read this book, you are destined for self-growth, which aligns with your higher purpose.

Here's another hidden lesson, and most self-help books skip it. I like to call it the Little Elephant in the self-help room...You see, it's not that the "traditional path" is always wrong. And it's not about becoming a rebel just for the sake of it.

It's all about being true to yourself and having the courage to adapt your path if needed.

Let me explain...as you've probably already noticed, self-help literature usually advocates entrepreneurship or self-employment. Spirituality books recommend following your passion and purpose to make a living. And these are great if that's your path. But spirituality and self-growth can be fulfilled on whatever professional path you are as long as you are true to yourself and feel good about your choices.

Sometimes people think they are following their own opinion when, in reality, they are not. For example, a person might leave a traditional path of having a steady 9-5 job to become an entrepreneur just because they have seen an online ad that promised God knows what. And so, they quit their job without even thinking twice about following a path that wasn't for them to begin with. It's not that everyone has to be an entrepreneur or a coach, or a healer.

It's about true self-discovery and creating your own way...

The more you talk to your subconscious mind using its language, the more you will learn about your true self and authentic desires...

The answers will be revealed to you. Just remember to tune in and keep asking good questions. That will optimize your inner search engines to give you the best information and results, all personalized to your needs.

A popular opinion, such as having a steady 9-5 office job (or a similar career path) may not be for you. Or it may be for you. You may be enjoying your workplace and the stability it provides.

An alternative self-help literature opinion to become a coach or a healer, or perhaps have an online business and travel the world may be for you, or it may not be for you.

Don't fall for the shiny object (popular or alternative). Instead, tune in and keep replaying your life map. In your mind, go deeply into various areas of life that are important to you and play them out the way you desire.

You see, this is what most people miss. They do it the other way around. They follow a popular or a cool/alternative opinion without ever going inwards and consulting their heart's desires. And then they wonder why things are not working out. Luckily, now you know better. Also, please remember to be good to yourself even if you get off track or get tempted by some shiny object, whether created by popular or alternative opinion or whatever opinion that wasn't aligned with your highest truth.

Sometimes, you need to test different things and options to learn your truth so never beat yourself up for trying and "failing". I think I've already told you that you don't fail, you succeed or you learn, right?

At the same time, it's about respecting other people's choices and beliefs.

It's not about convincing others to your point of view...

It's about acknowledging that there is an infinite amount of paths. Because there's no one set-in-stone definition of success.

If someone tells you their way is the best, and you should follow it, remember to protect your energy by not engaging in such a conversation and not providing any explanations. You don't have to explain your way. Simply embody it and live it.

You are the one who decides what's best for you. Your heart's desires are unique to you.

Look at what you have and who you are. It can be challenging, but you will get there with my help and the tools you have now.

Release your anger for not being true to yourself and believing everybody else more than yourself. Again, this is a part of your journey. Now, you know better, and your past mistakes are transmuted into your superpower!

You must decide very firmly and confidently to start your own game. The game where *only you* choose what to believe, think and do.

Be your best friend and lover. So, in every situation, especially a challenging one, be loving and patient with yourself.

Finally, when you fully embrace your own truth and begin to live it, don't forget that others have their own truths too. Everyone has value to share. Everyone can teach you something.

The fact that others have their own opinions doesn't mean you are not being heard, so don't take any perceived rejection personally. Remember that when you're entirely focused on being your best self and living your truth, you will attract more and more people on a similar journey. I say *similar* because, naturally, even those like-minded souls will have their own truths. And that's the beauty of life. Since everyone is different, we can interact, learn, share and grow. You will have many things in common that connect you and many things you do differently that allow you to grow, expand and enjoy different view points.

So, remember that staying grounded in your own truth while constantly developing your own definition of success is your new lifestyle...At the same time, encourage others to do the same and let them know that their view points matter and deserve to be heard.

As you live it fully and boldly, remember never to compare yourself with others and their achievements.

Here's where I, Your Higher Self, desire to help you. It's not about your achievements but about your journey and how much that journey lights you up. I used to say that it's about progress, and that's undoubtedly true to some extent...

But the problem is that sometimes you may start comparing your progress to that of others and forget that everyone is different...

So, let me repeat: it's not about how many achievements you had but about the journey you're on and how that journey transforms you and your well-being. That's my definition of success.

And what about yours, my beautiful Highest of the Highest Self?

Let me guide you through this process because it's not as simple as some quick scripting exercises (although these are great, and Elena has a book on scripting that can help you!).

It's about writing your own success playbook, your sacred success playbook! Like any book, it will take time.

Unlike any book, it will be a never-ending process of growth...

I am serious here. Get a journal and call it My Sacred Success Playbook. Or, create a folder on your device.

Write a few words or sentences daily to redefine who you are and create new boundaries and joyful rules to embody. How do you respond to life, and what do you do in different situations? The easiest way to create your own rules is to imagine you are teaching them to someone.

Create your own process, and stay consistent. After a few years, you'll have an amazing transformation and, if you want to, you will be a fantastic mentor to others who yet need to define who they are and what they truly desire.

Your sacred success playbook will help you save time on worry and doubt. You will create and embody new boundaries and new possibilities. So, how do you feel about writing your own playbook and creating a space where we can connect daily?

Your best self awaits you. And it's waiting to be fully embodied!

So how do you get started?

Every day, write a few sentences about lessons you learned. Or the challenges encountered and how you are transforming them. Print a few good headlines here and there as well!

Your New Self, your Higher Self, can't wait to read your personal book and rules for life. In a few years, it will make sense, and you will have tears of joy as you read your story of transformation. Start documenting it now in whatever way feels good to you. Private or public. Allow your inner compass and authenticity to guide you!

Chapter 3 - Lesson 3

Making Friends with Fear (Instead of Fighting It!). The Perfect Integration Process for Unlimited Courage.

Now you know how to empower yourself to follow yourself and create your best life. You also know how to team up with your subconscious mind in alignment with your heart's desires.

And so, you may be thinking: "But what about fear? How can I overcome it when I feel like it's blocking me and making me doubt myself and my goals?".

Let's change your mindset a bit...

Because asking how to fight, overcome or eliminate fear may be the wrong question that is not serving you...

What you need to understand first is how not to fear your fears. Your secret, love-based and peaceful "weapon" is called courage. The more courageous you intend to be, the less fear can control you.

So how about asking yourself this question: "How can I become more courageous?".

This mindset is similar to that of focusing on gratitude. When you use your energy to feel grateful, it's almost impossible to complain, right?

Well, when you focus on being courageous, your courage expands.

Similarly, be aware of different ups and downs in your inner state and always intend to investigate them from a place of love, curiosity, and peace.

Thanks to fear, you can appreciate the opposite state, which is courage. So, you can be grateful for your fears, and when you are grateful, you feel more at peace with yourself and can dive deeper to make some inner changes and focus on courage.

So, when you are afraid, promise yourself to confront your fears. Expose them, and you will unleash more and more courage.

Imagine this scenario: You invite your fear for a cup of coffee and let it speak, you hear it out. Don't tell it to shut up, and don't suppress it. Remember that thanks to your fear, the opposite, that is, your courage, also exists.

So, be in the mindset of making friends with your fear to get stronger.

If you keep avoiding your fear, it will keep knocking on your door when you least expect it, and chances are, it will keep getting noisier and noisier.

So, develop a mindful, peaceful and neutral relationship with fear. Also, give yourself some love and understanding. Fearing some goals and activities is normal, especially if you're new to them. Successful people are not totally fearless souls...

But they understand something; they know that fear is a part of their human existence, and there's nothing to fight or resist. What you resist persists.

Here's another beautiful mindset shift that will serve you: What you should really fear is not confronting your fear and not intending to live your full potential.

Maybe you fear going after a new job or changing your career path. But you can also direct your fear more wisely. You can fear lost opportunities and unexpressed talents...

You can fear not tapping into your full potential...

So how do you see fear now? Can you use it as your new friend to make you more courageous in pursuing your goals and dreams? Let's invite some of your fears for coffee...

For example, let's say you have a fear of starting your passion project or moving to a new city that offers better opportunities for you. Let's dive into that fear and embrace it fully...What would be the best and worst-case scenario? What do you really have to lose?

Invite your fear (or fears) for a cup of coffee now. The best way is to journal your thoughts and use them to guide you. Feel free to follow this process or something similar.

Example: *I fear moving to a new city, even though I know much better opportunities await me there...*

Best case scenario: *I move to a new city, pursue my new dream job and other goals, and become successful. I meet new friends and feel at home. I find more and more opportunities that were not available to me in my hometown.*

Worst case scenario- *I move to a new city and don't like it there. Things don't go as planned. So, I decide to move back home. But at least I tried and met some new people and made exciting connections. Who knows, maybe, I'll try again in the future; perhaps it wasn't the best timing for* me. *Still, I feel good about myself because I tried. Hmm...this "worst-case scenario" doesn't sound that bad. I just need to prepare myself and carefully research my options before moving there.*

Middle case scenario: *I move to a new city, but things are a bit slow. Still, I meet new people, attract great opportunities eventually, and develop my skills.*

Have you noticed that fear doesn't consume you that much once put on paper (aka invited for coffee)? You're no longer in your head; you see how many options you have. You can also see that the worst-case scenario isn't that bad. Now that you understand it, you can prepare to increase your chances of success.

So...if something holds you back, make peace with it.

Sooner or later, you will reach a stage where you will keep going, even when most people give up. And you will teach your success mindset to others. This process works for all industries and walks of life.

You can also look at things you feel skeptical about, some old limiting beliefs, triggers, or fears.

I'll give you a simple exercise you can do daily to start liberating yourself from whatever is holding you back. It consists of two simple steps. When you dive into it, you will wonder how you could ever live without it!

Step#1 Invite your fears, worries, or triggers for a cup of coffee. But not all of them at once. Invite them one by one.

In your journal, write exactly what you fear and why. What triggers that fear?

Step#2 Release your triggers and fears through meditation. All you need is a simple intention. You can also say: "I release and let it go". Meditate for as long as you need to. Remind yourself with each breath that you are breathing in new opportunities, love, and light. As you breathe out, remind yourself you are letting go of whatever it is that no longer serves you.

It may take a few rounds to release an old belief, limiting mindset, or whatever is holding you back. But now, you have the tools to take care of yourself and choose inner peace. With inner peace, it's much easier to attract new opportunities that serve you. This is why I encourage you to do this releasing exercise as a daily practice.

Everything seems hard in the beginning. But now you have the tools to be at peace with the unknown and keep growing stronger and stronger while still giving yourself the sense of security you deserve.

Remember that the purpose of fear is to propel you for what is yet to come. Don't interpret it as a reason not to get started on something you love.

Forget about being less fearful; instead, focus on using fear to be more courageous. You will feel both happy and fulfilled!

Fear doesn't have to control your life; just let it speak and use its words wisely to manifest your heart's desires.

Use courage to face fear and acceptance to transform fear into love.

Finally, acknowledge that fear can destroy everything you can be. If you can make peace with it, you can face anything.

So many people let their fears defeat them, making life sad for them. But now you know there's a better way, and you can use fear to encourage courage and let it guide you!

Now you have all the tools you need to become authentically successful and keep growing. This book is short for a reason...It's meant to be lived more than read...Because now, your main job is to fully embody what you've just learned and live your best life. Become living proof of what is possible when you transform your mindset and energy!

We can't wait to see how your story unfolds,

Thank You for reading to the very end,

With love and gratitude,

Elena & Your Beautiful Higher Self

PS. Final message from Your Higher Self:

"My beautiful Highest of my Highest Self. Your mind and heart are stronger than you can imagine. I believe in you fully. Emody, live, and breathe this little book as you keep writing your own! I am always here for you. And together we are stronger than ever. It's our time to shine. Our past made us stronger. Now we are wise, courageous, and authentic. We have everything we need to keep going while creating magic and abundance with each and every step we take.

Love – Love – Love

Thank You – Thank You – Thank You

+ big thanks to Elena for facilitating this conversation and giving our wisdom beautiful clothing of words that inspire, motivate and elevate!"

Until next time we connect, Your Higher Self ***

Join Our Manifestation Newsletter and Get a Free eBook

To help you amplify what you've learned in this book, I'd like to offer you a free copy of my LOA Workbook – a powerful, 5-day program (eBook & audio) designed to help you raise your vibration while eliminating resistance and negativity.

To sign up for free, visit the link below now:

www.loaforsuccess.com/newsletter

You'll also get free access to my inspirational LOA Newsletter to help you stay high vibe!

Through this email newsletter, I regularly share all you need to know about the manifestation mindset and energy.

Plus, whenever I release a new book, you can get it at a deeply discounted price.

To sign up for free, visit the link below or scan the code.

www.loaforsuccess.com/newsletter

If you happen to have any technical issues with your sign-up, please email us at:

support@LOAforSuccess.com

More by Elena

Now available on Amazon:

Manifesting Alignment: Secrets to Becoming a Vibrational Match to Your Desires

Manifestation Meditation: It's Time to Meditate to Attract Your Best Life (Because You Can!)

About Elena

Elena G. Rivers is a Law of Attraction & Self-Development author with a passion for helping ambitious souls manifest their dream reality. Elena focuses on combining her practical self-image & personal vibration tools with timeless metaphysical concepts to help you permanently shift your mindset and energy to create a new, more empowered version of yourself so that you can create the life you love, desire and deserve.

She's a big believer in - you don't attract what you want, you attract WHO you are. This is why mindset and energy work are so important! After all, we want long-term success and fulfillment and we want to be able to manifest over and over again with joy and ease!

Through her highly inspirational and practical books such as *How Not to Manifest, Visualization Demystified, Script to Manifest,* and *Speak to Manifest,* Elena has helped thousands of people across the globe find inner peace, empowerment, success, and abundance. It's all about making metaphysical concepts easy-to-apply to get the results you want.